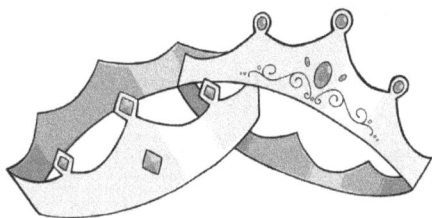

To contact the authors, please go to RoyalCouple.com.

Published in the United States of America by 501 Videos LLC

Cover Design: Christopher Davenport
Interior Layout: Bryan Tomasovich
Illustration: Suzy Claflin
Photo: Benjamin Davenport

Davenport, Stephanie & Christopher

Royal Couple: How the story of one couple's accidental discovery of "King and Queen Days" can lead you to a "happily ever after" marriage.

First Edition
ISBN 978-1-7350374-0-0

Also for sale in ebook format.

1. Family & Relationships / Marriage & Long-Term Relationships
2. Family & Relationships / Conflict Resolution
3. Family & Relationships / Love & Romance

Printed in the U.S.A.

Royal Couple

How the story of one couple's accidental discovery
of "King and Queen Days" can lead you
to a "happily ever after" marriage.

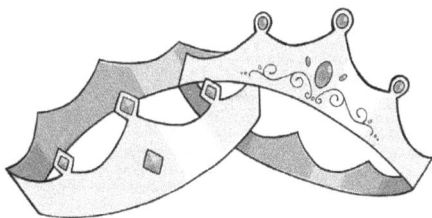

A simple guide to a
more loving and happier partnership

STEPHANIE & CHRISTOPHER DAVENPORT

Contents

The 10 Words
That Saved Our Marriage

It was only 10 words.

Ten simple words that saved our marriage.

Hi. I'm Steph.

I'm coming out of my introverted shell to tell you about this because every single person my husband, Chris, and I have told our story to is fascinated.

Their eyes light up, they lean into to hear more, a quiet stillness settles over them. They see the promise and potential these ten words offer their partnership.

These ten words came out of my husband's mouth in the middle of an unusual and unexpected week-long snowstorm that trapped us inside our home.

Together.

You see, Chris and I were engaged two and a half weeks after we met and married five weeks later. Yep, you did the math right. Within eight weeks of meeting, we were legally bound, sharing a small studio apartment, a bed, and a bank account.

It was during those first rain-soaked spring months in Seattle that we started to get to really know each other.

We were about as compatible as oil and water.

I was tidy. He was…less tidy.

He was generous with his money. I was frugal.

I liked the security of a job. He liked the excitement of entrepreneurship.

He wanted to have kids. I was not so sure about parenthood.

He expressed his feelings immediately and loudly (which to me felt unkind and bullish). I shared my feelings after quiet, careful, and prolonged consideration (which to him felt dishonest and deceptive).

Neither of us felt safe, understood, or appreciated.

Why did we stay together, you may ask.

Stupidity. Stubbornness. Curiosity…and some good times.

We found we both valued family and marriage. If you were

to look at a photo album of our lives together, you would see us horseback riding with Chris' family at the ocean, dressed as pirates at my family's yearly chaotic reunion called, "Camp-Run-Amok," camping with dear friends at our favorite lake, sledding with cousins in the mountains....

And, yet beneath these good times, there was tension between us.

We both wondered if we should divorce.

We put the option of divorce on the table between us more than once. It always came down to, "I love you, damn it!" And we would sigh deeply, square our shoulders, and trudge on. Year after year after year after year.

We watched our two inquisitive, rambunctious boys grow into responsible, thoughtful, self-sufficient teenagers, we worked long days (and nights) building a successful small business, we watched our parents age, we sometimes wondered if we were going be able to pay the mortgage, we disagreed about everything (yes, everything from money, to parenting, to sex, to politics, to household chores, to business direction, whether we should even have our own business.... And, don't get me started about the dogs).

One thing we did agree on—that our marriage was really hard.

All twenty-five years of it.

What ten words could possibly change all of that?

I'll tell you.

These are the ten words that came out of Chris' mouth that snowy afternoon....

"I want to serve you...you know, like a Queen."

And he meant it!

Those ten words started us on an interesting journey.

A journey that led a local shop owner to assume Chris and I were newlyweds.

And, at our neighborhood grocery store, a complete stranger, who overheard us giggling in the checkout line, leaned over and said, "You two belong together."

And the fun thing is, after twenty-five years in a difficult marriage, we do feel like newlyweds. And we do feel like we belong together.

Finally.

This small book shows you how these ten words started us on an unexpected journey. A journey that, within a few months, wiped away years of mistrust, resentments, and blame, while revealing the sweet relationship we'd been dreaming of for decades.

Perhaps this journey will reveal your dream relationship.

The Beginning
of the Journey

A weeklong snowstorm raged outside.

Divorce clouds loomed inside.

Chris and I were stuck together.

We happily avoided each other during this snowstorm.

That is until Chris came up to me as I was reading peacefully on the couch.

This was the moment our marriage started to change for the better.

Chris stood before me and said...

"I want to serve you...you know, like a Queen."

I blink at him.

He says, "Is there anything I can do for you?"

I can't quite think of anything, so I say, "I'm good."

Chris disappears into another room in the house.

A couple of hours later, Chris comes back and asks, "Is there anything I can do for you? Would you like a cup of tea?"

I actually did want a cup of tea. He happily made me tea. That may be the second or third cup of tea he has made me in our entire twenty-five-year marriage.

For the remaining three days of our snowy seclusion, Chris was dedicated to serving me. He made me countless cups of tea, cooked one of my favorite meals, offered to give me a foot massage….

He was genuinely willing and happy to serve.

I started to lean into this fun game of his, to let him take care of me.

This felt a bit alien. I'm always the one taking care of others.

I rarely think about what I want.

But now, I find myself asking, "What do I want?"

I didn't get a chance to go deep with this question because the weather warmed up and Chris cooled down. Way down.

Here's what happened on the fourth day.

Chris woke up on the wrong side of the bed and got surlier as the day wore on.

It was just a matter of time before the storm clouds came rumbling to a head and the lightening flashed.

To give you a little history, our typical argument pattern proceeds as follows:

Chris lets me know everything I have ever done wrong since time began, and exactly how selfish I am, and how critical I am, and how hard he has worked for our family, and how I never prioritize him, and how he never gets his needs met.

I, in turn, ask him not to yell at me.

He's not yelling, he informs me, he's expressing his feelings loudly.

Then I proceed to explain to him a more effective way to communicate with me so I can actually hear him without feeling degraded and defensive. (This, by the way, does NOT help the situation).

And, for the record, I am not being critical of his communication style; I'm "helping" him be a better communicator. My "helping" Chris left him feeling disrespected, degraded, and unheard.

So, on this fourth day, Chris and I find each other in the kitchen after a morning of responding to emails from customers, clients, and colleagues.

I decide I might as well get this particular storm over with. I cautiously open Pandora's box.

"So…what's going on?"

The downpour begins.

At the bottom of the "Litany of Steph's Inexcusable Sins" is the final recent affront:

"Over the last few days you never once asked me what I wanted!"

Those words hung in the air awhile before I could respond.

"I honestly didn't know that was part of the game," I reply. "I thought you wanted to know what I wanted. I didn't know you wanted me to ask you the same thing!"

Chris' shoulders slump.

Three facts become undeniably clear:

1. (Communication style aside) Chris is right. I didn't ask him what he wanted.
2. This interesting "Serve you like a Queen" game is going to continue beyond our snowy reprieve.
3. This game needs to be equal between us so that we can both be nurtured.

Chris says, "How about you be Queen for another week?"

"No way!" I reply. "I'm not stepping into that trap again. You'll get resentful. How about you be King tomorrow and I'll be Queen the next day. We'll alternate days after that."

Chris' shoulders un-slump.

In fact, there is a noticeable gleam in his eye.

And that's how Queen and King Days began.

Within two weeks of alternating between King and Queen Days, we found ourselves happier and more loving toward each other.

It just made sense to continue.

Before we knew it, we'd been on this unexpected Queen and King journey for over a year—the happiest year of our marriage!

We've broken this journey down into a few simple steps and examples to help you on your way to a happier, more loving, and playful partnership. These steps can be used even if you are retired, a busy working couple, or still in the very active phase of raising small children. In fact, I wish we had these tools when we were raising small children!

Chris and I would have had a solid framework to help prioritize each other and make unified decisions during chaotic times.

It's so easy.

Embarrassingly simple.

You'll see.

The Steps Along the Royal Road

The first year of practicing Queen and King Days was one of our busiest years ever. Our business grew. We sent our oldest son off to college. And, we helped Chris' dad through the end stages of a fatal illness.

One of us always remembered if it was a King Day or a Queen Day.

We met each other daily.

We supported each other.

We enjoyed each other.

And we laughed more than in all of our previous years of marriage combined.

How did we get to the marriage we've always dreamed of?

We unknowingly followed 5 simple steps.

You can use these same 5 steps as guides on your journey to a happier marriage:

1. Check in With Your Partner
2. Help Your Partner Get What They Need and Want
3. Ask for What You Need and Want
4. Take Turns Giving and Receiving
5. Reduce Arguments by Using Fun Ways to Think About Each Other

That's it.

The following chapters walk you through these steps.

The first step may surprise you.

Checking in with your partner is a sneaky way of freeing yourself of the responsibility of your partner's expectations.

On Your Terms

Before we move on to the first step, there are a few things for you to think about as you go through this book.

With the unexpected discovery of King and Queen Days, there came the days where the "non-ruling spouse" ended up in a "servant" type supportive role.

We know "servant" often has a negative connotation. Instead, imagine an invaluable and respected member of the household.

That's the kind of servant role we are talking about.

There are other names for individuals who serve and support royalty: chamberlain, courtier, Privy Council, groom, lady-in-waiting, steward, constable, master or mistress of the household…pick one that works for you.

Throughout this book, we refer to the "Loyal Servant of the Day" and the "Dignified Servant of the Day" interchangeably. We also use the term "servant" with a lighthearted approach, not as a literal servant.

Chris and I discovered we both LOVE being in the "servant" role every other day. It's actually pretty relaxing not being in charge.

You'll see.

Also note, if you are uncomfortable with the title of Queen/King and Loyal/Dignified Servant, or you prefer gender neutral terms that more accurately reflect your partnership, change them!

You can be captain and sailor, pilot and steward, president and vice president, team lead and team support, conductor and musician, director and assistant director, producer and production assistant, coach and athlete, lead actor and supporting cast, rock star and roadie…it really doesn't matter what language you use as long as the roles of lead and support person are established.

We use Queen/King because that's how it accidentally showed up for us. We happen to have a lot of fun with these titles and the language that royalty inspires. You'll see samples of this later in the "Royal Lexicon" chapter.

Step 1

Check in with Your Partner

Believe it or not, the first step to a happier marriage is to check in with your partner.

Yep, it's true.

Checking in will lead to a happier you, a happier spouse and a happier marriage.

Here is what you do.

Go up to your spouse and ask, "Is there anything I can do for you?"

Then just stand there and wait.

While you stand there, empty your mind of all the things you need to do, and all problems you have at work. Take a mental break from all the demands of your life.

Your whole job right now is to be present for your partner for those few seconds.

That's all.

Your partner may look at you dumbfounded. That's ok.

This may take awhile for them to get used to.

If they answer and tell you what you can do for them, DO IT. And do it willingly. Preferably with a smile on your face.

They may want a drink of water, or a cup of coffee.

Get it for them.

Now, is your mind screaming, "What about what I want?!"

It's ok. We'll get to that.

Are you thinking about all of the things you need to get done?

I did too. They'll get done. You'll see.

Let's put this into action.

Before you read further, go up to your spouse and ask them,

"Is there anything I can do for you?"

Go ahead. Do this now. Even if you are busy. It really

doesn't' take a lot of time to show up for your partner for a few seconds.

I'll wait....

If you and/or your partner are at work, shoot your partner a text or give them a quick call, if possible.

Ask them if there is anything you can do for them that will help their evening go a bit smoother. Is there anything you can do for them that will make their homecoming that much sweeter?

Did your spouse ask you to do something? Do it.

Great! Then go ask, "Is there anything else I can do for you?"

And wait. Take your mental break.

If they say no, that's great, too. You can go on to your to-do list. Happily.

In about an hour or so, go ask your spouse or partner again, "Hey, I'm heading to the kitchen, is there anything I can get for you?"

Then just get it for them. Happily.

How do you feel? Pretty good, huh?

And, your partner is probably feeling a little bit cared for and prioritized without even knowing why.

Good job!

Here's the other thing: without even knowing it, you just relieved yourself of all responsibilities and expectations in your relationship. You just gave your partner the power to ask for what they want. That's a HUGE break for you, by the way.

You can thank my husband, Chris, for this. It was his idea.

He pulled this sneaky trick on me over a year ago.

He will tell you what happened….

When I told Steph that I wanted to serve her like a Queen, I wasn't trying to be chivalrous.

I wasn't even trying to be nice.

I was just plain tired.

We had recently hosted a group of business colleagues at our farmhouse for a few days. As an introvert, that kind of prolonged interaction, along with the endless responsibility of running a business, left me depleted and exhausted.

I didn't want to talk.

I didn't want to think.

I didn't want to make one more decision. Or exert one more brain cell.

I especially did not want to try to guess what Steph was expecting of me that day.

I was done.

D.O.N.E.

So, I selfishly put the whole day in Steph's hands by offering to serve her...like a Queen.

All day.

So, I asked her:

"Is there anything I can do for you?"

And then I let my mind go blank. I didn't have to think. She was in charge. It was now in her hands to tell me what she needed. I didn't have to try and guess.

I could finally relax.

Sigh.

At first, Steph just stared at me from her cozy perch on the couch. I could practically see the gears turning in her head. *What is THIS all about?*

I waited. Ready to do anything she desired.

She narrowed her eyes at me. "I'm good," she said. And she went back to reading her book.

I was dismissed.

I was free.

FREE!

I didn't have to do a single thing in that moment.

I went up to my office, sat down in my favorite chair, and simply watched the snow fall.

That's all I did. Surrounded by thick, white silence.

Did you see what he did? He got himself off the hook!

It worked too.

I just thought he was being really, really nice.

And I liked it! Brilliant!

Let's move on to step 2.

Step 2

Help Your Partner Get What They Need and Want

The next phase of developing your happier marriage is to go a bit deeper with your partner.

In addition to showing up throughout the day and asking, "Is there anything I can do for you?", help your partner get more of their needs met.

Your partner is probably not used to asking for what they want, so you can prompt them a little.

For example, you can say, "Hey, it looks like we have Thursday evening available, is there anything you would really like to do? A concert? A movie? I'm all yours."

And you wait. Relax. Give yourself a much-deserved break. Be fully present for your partner. Your partner can feel this focused energy.

Here's another example of what you can say: "I know you've been working really hard. Can I give you a shoulder massage?"

And you wait. Breath. Enjoy your partner.

You'll notice when you support your partner in these extra ways, they will soften a bit toward you.

You'll see.

Your spouse is now beginning to get the subliminal message that you are their partner in getting their needs and wants met, not the barrier to getting their needs and wants met.

Did you catch that? Read that last paragraph again.

Do you see the subtle shift that is happening?

This is subtle yet HUGE.

So, keep it up!

Step 3

Ask for What You Need and Want

It's your turn!

The next step to a happy partnership is to actually ask for what you need and want.

Easier said than done.

Why?

You might have a hard time asking for what you need and want.

You may not know what you want.

Maybe you don't feel like you deserve what you need and want.

Maybe you don't think your partner can deliver what you need and want.

You may not have enough time to get what you need and want.

Or all of the above.

Sometimes it's hard to know what you want when you are so used to serving others.

Start by asking for little things: food, drinks, small acts of service like making the bed or preparing part of a meal.

That's what I did.

And, I asked myself, "When do I feel really loved?" This helped me discern what I need and want.

I also noticed that when I was feeling angry or sad, there was often an unmet need or unconscious expectation. I realized I had to listen to those feelings and be honest with myself in order to clearly communicate my needs with Chris.

While I had a hard time advocating for my needs, Chris, on the other hand, was always asking for what he needed and wanted.

I knew what Chris' needs were. I heard what he said. I just did not understand his needs because his needs were opposite of mine.

And, I'll be honest.

I was also refusing to meet Chris' needs out of spite. I was thinking, "You're not meeting my needs, why should I meet yours?!"

But, he couldn't meet my needs because I did not communicate what my needs were. Duh!

Whether we ask or not, we still need what we need, and want what we want.

Those needs and wants are still there, year, after year, after year.

So, here's what you could do...

Throw a tizzy fit.

You'll remember that's what Chris did when he listed all of my defects then said, "Over the last few days you never once asked me what I want!"

I don't recommend that.

Instead, follow Chris' other tactic.

He'll tell you how he prepared me to get his needs met. This happened on the night before his first official King Day.

Steph and I crawl into bed after an emotionally and mentally draining day of work.

I ask softly, "Is there anything I can do for you before we fall asleep?"

Steph sighs and says, "*Hmmm....*"

"Do you want me to rub your feet?" I ask.

I admit it.

It was a strategic question.

I know that Steph loves to have her feet rubbed. I also know that a foot massage reliably delivers her into an altered state of consciousness. She would give up national security secrets while under the influence of a gently caressed pinky toe. I'm not after security secrets. But, I do need to give her a fair warning about my first King Day.

She rotates herself on the bed and puts her feet onto my stomach.

"Yes, please! A foot rub would be wonderful," she says.

I touch her left big toe and her eyes roll back into some bliss-filled place. I pull out some mint-scented lotion I had hidden under the pillow. I rub it slowly into the ball of her foot.

Steph's breathing deepens. There is a bit of drool at the corner of her mouth.

"So, um…about King Day…" I begin.

She nods ever so slightly and licks her lips.

"I want to apologize in advance."

I move my fingers to the arch of her foot with smooth deliberate strokes.

She moans.

"I may be pretty selfish on King Days."

Long strokes on her ankles and calves.

"*Uh huh*," she exhales.

I slide my hands gently back to her toes to finish her left foot.

"But only in the beginning," I assure her.

"*Ahhhhh…*" she sighs.

"Just for the first couple of weeks," I conclude.

"OK…whatever…you…want," she says.

I squeeze more lotion into my hand and caress the pinky toe of her right foot.

Steph's breathing deepens even more. She will be asleep soon.

Then I can plan my King Day.

Do you see his genius mind?

He got me to happily agree to meet his needs by giving me mine!

I felt like he was supporting me and looking out for me. How could I not return the favor?

So simple. So obvious.

It worked too.

Which leads us to Step 4 of the master plan.

Step 4

Take Turns
Giving and Receiving

You may have learned this fourth step in kindergarten.

Your kindergarten teacher probably said to your class, "Take turns children."

Queen and King Days create a place where both partners can get their varied needs met.

On one day we get to ask for what we need. On the next day we serve and give our partner what they need.

Ask and receive. Then give and serve. Repeat.

You may ask, *Every single day?*

YES!

Prioritizing one another is an ongoing daily practice. If you skip a day or two, you lose momentum. Then you are right back where you started.

And, why wait to get your needs met?

On the off day you chose not to ask for what you want on your royal day, because of obligations, time constraints, or some other reason, guess what, another royal day is coming, soon!

You will get your turn.

That knowledge in itself relaxes both partners. It's an agreement that promises I will get my needs met. If not today, then tomorrow.

Because Chris and I consistently alternate between King Day and Queen Day, we found we were able to relax into each other. We finally trusted that we would show up for one another.

Although…I almost bailed on Chris.

Here's how Chris' first official King Day unfolded.

I called it the "Reign of Terror."

Before we get into why I call it the Reign of Terror, you need to know that one of the many areas where Chris and I vary is physical affection.

Your partnership may have a variation of this same theme.

Chris likes a LOT of hugging, touching, caressing, kissing n'stuff. Me? Not so much. In fact, I feel a bit smothered sometimes. Almost like I can't breathe.

It's been a HUGE problem for us.

The more affectionate Chris was, the more distant I became. When I started feeling antsy, smothered, and well past the "dessert portion" of a meal, Chris was just beginning his appetizer. We both left the table unsatisfied. I was overly stuffed and Chris was starving.

In twenty-five years of marriage, we still had not come upon a solution to this particular feast/famine dilemma.

So…I'll just say it.

I was NOT looking forward to King Day.

I felt a little like a warrior going into battle not knowing if I would survive. Or a scuba diver who doesn't know if their air tank is big enough for the dive ahead.

But, the job had to be done.

Fair is fair (and he did give me an awesome foot rub).

The first officially mandated King Day started as our usual days do….

Our two dogs, a perpetually starving Beagle named Shadow, and a large, perpetually shedding Malamute named Kona, remind me who the boss really is as they paw the sliding glass door to be released into the backyard to take care of their official and imperative morning business.

I look over to see that Chris is sound asleep.

I climb out of bed and stumble through the kitchen. I let the dogs outside. I click on the electric teakettle and wait for the water to boil for my morning cup of tea. I grab my favorite mug from the cupboard.

Something is different.

Something is very, very wrong.

I pause with a mug in one hand and a tea bag in the other.

Then, I remember.

Oh Crap! It's "King Day."

I pour hot water into my cup and set the timer. It dawns on me that while Chris was rubbing my feet last night, I may have agreed to something that is not in my best interest. Did I actually agree to do whatever he wanted?

What does "Whatever you want..." mean, anyway? Pole dancing? Slinky uncomfortable, unbecoming cheetah-print lingerie? Bacon? Pole dancing with bacon?

The tea timer beeps.

I quickly and quietly silence the timer.

I strain to hear any movement from the bedroom.

Nothing. I sigh.

Then the toilet flushes.

I freeze.

His Majesty is awake.

Ahhh! What's the protocol on King Day?

What do I do?

How do I serve a king?

What should be my attitude?

What energy do I carry into the room?

Can I even do this?

Chris was my only compass here. During our snowy reprieve, Chris served me like a Queen. He was gracious and accommodating. He'd say stuff like, "Whatever you want." AND HE MEANT IT! He was available and willing to go with the flow of what I wanted to do. I noticed, with his attitude, I started to loosen up and relax and ENJOY being around him.

This was a new development in our relationship (sad but true). Usually, there was second-guessing, tension, unstated and unmet expectations, and lots and lots of resentment.

Would serving him help?

What Chris was asking me to step into felt different and fun.

He was demonstrating service in a way that made my insides feel soft, open, and vulnerable.

I want to do that for him. But, I'm not sure I can. I'm afraid.

I walk down the hall to our bedroom door. I realize what I am afraid of.

I'm afraid I will be devoured.

I'm afraid he wants more from me than I have to give. Then what?

I guess we'll find out.

With a cup of hot tea in hand, I square my shoulders, take a deep breath, and put my hand on the doorknob….

I'm happy to report that Chris did not have a single article of cheetah-print lingerie waiting for me, nor a pole for dancing.

PHEW!

The Royal Bedroom did have a very, very sweet King. There was lots of snuggling, kissing, and caressing (and other stuff).

After the third hour, I did get twitchy and seriously fought the urge to run screaming out of the room, down the stairs, out the front door, and down the dirt driveway to amaze the neighbors with all of my jiggling, naked glory.

Chris, recognizing my subtle signs of impending hysteria, granted me a royal pardon for a few hours.

Chris had a sweet smile on his lips, a soft gentleness in his eyes, and a completely relaxed body.

He was full. His meal was finally satisfying.

So that's what he has needed all of these years!

And, I learned, I wouldn't die (or suffocate) showing up for him.

I also learned that when I prioritized Chris, instead of my long to-do list, he could and would be fulfilled. And, everything on my to-do list would still get done. With that knowledge, I relaxed into and focused on Chris without that pesky list interfering.

What a relief! Chris' need for me always seemed huge, daunting, and urgent. Now, he is satisfied. He can trust me to show up, so he is calm and content.

It seems that we stumbled upon a way of being where we BOTH could ask for and get what we need (and want).

One Royal Day at a time.

And, tomorrow is a Queen Day....

Before we go onto Step 5, let me tell you about my ultimate Queen Day.

I'm telling you this so that you too can start thinking about what your ideal royal day looks like.

And then, I'm going to share the three steps I took to get to my ultimate day.

My ultimate Queen Day was a day I'd always wanted, but never allowed myself to have. I hesitate to share it with you because it was pretty uneventful.

On a Queen Day I took a day trip by myself.

I booked a room at an oceanside retreat complete with a

kitchenette. I wanted to prepare and eat my own simple meals alone....

I spent one glorious night and day alone.

I woke up to the distant roar of the ocean. I stretched out in a bed of clean, crisp sheets under a thick white comforter and listened to the waves.

I didn't have to get up. There were no dogs to let out, emails to answer, or meetings to attend. Chris was at home taking care of that for me. He had cleared the calendar so that I could have the entire Queen Day to myself.

I could roll over and fall back asleep if I wanted to. I wanted to.

But, I couldn't. I was too excited!

The vast guiltless hours of nothing were calling me. That, and a hot cup of strong black tea along with an English muffin and orange marmalade.

I took all morning to eat my breakfast snuggled up on the couch with my journal and a good book.

In the afternoon, I enjoyed a long walk on the sandy beach with only the wind and the seagulls as my companions.

I returned from my windy walk and took a nap!

An introvert's heaven.

When my quiet day ended, I headed home to my loving family fully rested, nourished, and recharged.

That was the gift of my Ultimate Queen Day.

Queen Days give me permission to have the kind of day I truly need.

In the past, I would feel so guilty for wanting to be away from my family and obligations. Sometimes, Chris would be resentful that I wanted to be away. He couldn't really understand. His needs are quite different than mine.

So, I never took the time for myself that I needed and wanted.

Chris is not resentful anymore. He gets it. Heck, he helps make my ideal Queen Days happen! We both know we will get what we need and want, because we help each other get it!

What used to be a power struggle is now a gift to one another.

Here are the three tricky hurdles I had to overcome:

1. I constantly denied my needs and wants.
2. I believed my family would suffer if I took care of myself.
3. I felt selfish when I took time for myself.

And the three steps I took to overcome these hurdles:

1. I acknowledged my needs and wants were valid.
2. I accepted that taking care of myself was also taking care of my family.
3. I understood that time for myself was necessary, not selfish.

What will you do with your Ultimate Royal Day?

Step 5

Reduce Arguments by Using Fun Ways to Think About Each Other

The final step will show you how using fun ways to think about each other can dissolve arguments and encourage playfulness.

Do you and your partner have the same argument over and over and over again?

We did. It's pretty darn exhausting, right?

But now, Chris and I use royal language in thinking and speaking.

This lets us take things a little less seriously.

We smile and laugh a lot more.

Instead of butting heads and attacking each other, Chris and I speak through our roles as King or Queen.

It's surprising how these silly roles take the emotional charge out of the conversation.

Here's a fun little story that happened to Chris and me within the first few months of our Queen and King Day experiment....

Once upon a time on a King Day, the King was not amused.

His servant was not quite grasping the finer points of her role of "Loyal Servant of the Day."

She outright said "NO!" to one of his plans in the morning. Then, when she offered to make dinner, she was not at the dinner table with their delicious meal at the agreed upon time. There was no hint of a meal being prepared in the kitchen. After an ardent search, the King found her in the garden, covered with dirt, planting cantaloupe seeds.

His Highness was very hungry.

The not so loyal servant, upon seeing his Majesty standing outside the garden gate, exclaimed, "Oops!" She dropped her gardening tools and skedaddled to the kitchen to prepare their evening meal.

Doing his best to quell his displeasure, the King ate his dinner in silence.

He needed time to think.

How does one best handle such careless disobedience without a guillotine, a dungeon, or a whipping post? How does one inspire the desired behavior without expressing feelings loudly and unintentionally demeaning the subject sitting before him?

The King thought and chewed and thought and chewed.

After the dinner settled in his stomach and the plates were removed, the King cleared his throat and asked, "What exactly went through your mind from the time you offered to make dinner to ending up in the garden? I'm not criticizing, I'm just curious."

"Well…ok," said the servant feeling a little exposed.

She took a deep breath.

"It's like this; I went to water the transplanted ferns out by the shed before starting to make dinner. On the way to the ferns, I saw the little broccoli and pea plants we bought were wilting in their containers. They also needed to be watered. Well, the hose is by the garden. So, I brought them out to the garden. Then I thought, why water them in their container? They will just dry out quicker. They really need to be planted. It will only take a few minutes. Since I'm planting the peas and broccoli, I might as well quickly plant the seeds for the cantaloupe, beans, lettuce, radishes, and carrots. It will only take a few minutes. Then I can water everything all together: the ferns, the vegetables, and the seeds. It will be more efficient that way."

"More efficient," repeated the King, tapping his fingers on the table.

"Yes! And, there is a cute little baby rabbit living under the shed," said the servant.

The King was silent, though his fingers continued to tap the table.

The King and servant's sixteen-year-old son came home and entered the kitchen just in time to hear the King say, "Here is what is going through my brain right now. You offered to make us dinner. We agreed upon a time and location. You left to make dinner. You got sidetracked. Instead of keeping YOUR agreement with me, you ended up planting seeds. Seeds are therefore more important to you than I am. On your list of priorities for the day, I rank below cantaloupe seeds."

It appears so, thought the servant.

That's what happens all of the time. The servant constantly tries to check little things off of her to-do list instead of spending time with the King.

She keeps pushing him down to the bottom of the to-do list.

OH MY GOD! THAT'S what King Chris means when he says, *I'm always at the bottom of your list*. He's been saying that for years! A looooooong time before he was King. OOPS!

"Thank you for sharing that with me," said the servant with complete sincerity. "That really helps."

At that comment, the sixteen-year-old son peeks out from behind the open refrigerator door. "Is this scripted?" he asked. "I mean, you call this a fight? What about arguing? What about defending yourself?"

"There is nothing to defend. Your dad is right," the servant replied. "Sorry kid. Hate to disappoint you."

I finally saw for myself what Chris had been trying to tell me for over two decades.

This was going to call for a whole new attitude of prioritizing Chris and a new way of thinking.

This use of playful thinking, as King and Not So Loyal Servant, led Chris and me to "fight" in an entirely different way. If you even want to call the cantaloupe seed incident a fight.

This "not prioritizing Chris" argument had been replayed in our marriage over and over and over again.

In the past, we would criticize each other's actions. This would put us both on the defensive. It was hard, if not impossible, to connect when we were guarding ourselves against the other.

But this time was different.

With Chris and me taking turns leading the day, I got to see how I was not playing my role as a trusted servant. It wasn't personal. There was nothing to defend. If the roles were reversed and Chris got sidetracked, I could call attention to his role, not his personality.

For us, it is so much easier to communicate and hear each other's grievances through roles of Queen/King and servant.

This way of thinking about each other as Royalty and Servant allows us fun ways to connect and dissolves those sticky arguments.

Speaking of sticky arguments, here's another way I navigate them....

When I need to bring up a touchy topic with Chris, I make sure to do it on a Queen Day. I tell Chris in advance how I want him to respond. If I want his feedback, I will ask for it.

Usually, I just want to be heard.

If Chris has a problem with what I've said, or how I ask him to respond, he can address it on his King Day. I'll happily listen. Even if he expresses his feelings loudly, it's ok. It's his day.

This works like a charm.

We really get to listen to each other's perspectives and have time to digest them before responding.

The next chapters go into greater detail of the role of the Loyal/Dignified Servant and the Gracious Queen and King.

Your Role
as a Dignified Servant

If you're like me, the idea of being a servant is not appealing.

I feel like I'm already a servant at work, with the kids, around the house, with the pets, in the yard, and with other social responsibilities.

More of that? No thanks. I'll pass.

But, then there is the idea of the Dignified, or Loyal Servant.

A Dignified/Loyal Servant, in my mind, is a well-paid, respected, and indispensable member of the household. This proud, butler-type individual is relied upon to create a smooth, organized, and hospitable environment for all involved. They specifically carry out the expressed wishes of the owner of the house. The owner of the house, in our case, is the Queen or King of the day.

Even with this definition in mind, I admit, I was slow to learn the servant role.

I like to be in control. I also know what's best for everyone. So...just get out of my way and no one will get hurt.

Did I mention the role of the servant did not come easily?

Chris, however, was good at it.

When I asked him about his view of the role of Loyal Servant of the Day, here's what he said:

"On Queen Days, my job is to serve you in a way that lets you know you are the most important person in my life. You are my first priority. I truly want you to have the best day possible. I always ask myself, what can I do to make your day as stress-free and joyful as possible?"

Chris does a fantastic job. On Queen days, I feel prioritized, fully supported, and loved.

To that end, the Dignified Servant of the Day's duty is to:

1. Check in at the beginning of the day to find out the Queen/King's schedule and plans.
2. Knowing the Queen/King's schedule and plans, find ways to make their day go as smoothly as possible.
3. Check in throughout the day to see if there's anything to do to make the King/Queen's day even better.
4. Notice surprising and fun ways to go above and beyond to delight the King or Queen.
5. Check in at the end of the day to see if there is anything else needed or wanted.

Chris will tell you what usually happens on a Queen Day:

"On Queen Days, I get up to take care of the dogs. When Steph wakes up, I bring her a cup of tea in bed. I crawl back into bed with her and we snuggle (Steph likes to snuggle now) and talk quietly until the alarm goes off. Steph takes a shower. I'm not a big believer in wasting energy making a bed; however, on Queen Days, I make the bed for Steph. I know she loves that. I then ask Steph about her plans for the day. I ask her how I can help her achieve her goals for the day. Is there anything else she needs? Then we go about our day. I check in a couple of times to see if there is anything she needs or wants. I may just go into her office and give her a sweet kiss. At the end of the work day, I'll ask if there is anything she's craving for dinner. If yes, I'll do my best to make it for her. Barring any evening meetings or plans, we'll spend the evening however Steph wants. Before we go to bed, I will ask if there is anything I can do for her. Does she want a foot rub…?"

On King Days, the roles are reversed. Here's what I do for Chris:

I quietly get up and take care of the dogs. When I hear Chris stirring, I go in to see if there is anything I can get for him: a cup of tea or a mocha. I get him what he requests. I crawl back into bed with him and snuggle until the alarm goes off. After his shower, I ask him about his plans for the day. I also ask how I can help him achieve his goals for the day. Does he need me to provide lunch for his meeting? Is there anything else he needs? Then we go about our day. I'll check in a couple of times with him to see if there is anything I can do for him. I may just go into his office and give him a kiss or a shoulder rub. When he walks by my office, I may lift up my shirt just to surprise him. At the end of the day, I'll ask if there is anything he is craving for dinner. If so, I'll do my best to make it. Barring any evening meetings or plans, we'll spend the evening however Chris wants. I'll ask once again before I go to bed, if there is anything I can do for him.

Our days are smooth and easy.

It wasn't always this way.

A few months into the Queen and King Day experiment, I was still having a hard time in the servant role....

I woke up on the next King Day determined to prioritize Chris above all else.

I did great, too…until he woke up.

By then I had two cups of coffee, read three chapters of an inspiring book, wrote several pages in my journal, and came up with a great solution to a problem I'd been having at work. I couldn't wait to share all of this with him!

I knew he liked to rest quietly.

I knew better than to barrage his Majesty with words in the morning.

I knew better than to bombard him with questions.

I knew he liked to ease slowly into his day.

I knew all of this.

And yet, old habits are hard to break. I was in bed with him less than two minutes before all of the caffeinated words came pouring out of my mouth.

And that is why, after putting up with my fountain of words for a full ten minutes, his Majesty got up from bed and announced, "I'm done. I don't want to talk about business in bed! I'm done. I don't want to talk about anything in bed and you missed all of my cues! I'm done! I'm going to work."

He stomped off to take a shower.

So, there I was. Dumbfounded.

I slumped in bed. I listened to the shower and waited for the inevitable.

In the past, Chris would hold his thick anger all day and give me a cold shoulder until he could sort out his mood. By evening, we would attempt to talk like civilized human beings. There's a whole day shot to hell.

My brain alternated between being defensive and recognizing I'd fumbled again.

In the past, I'd already be dressed and cleaning something, anything, that I could control. My marriage may be falling to pieces, but by god, the house would be clean.

This time, instead of getting up and cleaning, I stayed in bed.

Would I ever get King Days right? I screwed it up already. Am I doomed? NO! This is silly. I'm gonna make mistakes. I have new tools to work with. I can do this.

The day is not over.

What can I do, at this moment, to prioritize Chris?

I can still be present to what Chris wants.

I know Chris appreciates my naked form. The feminine image is a type of nourishment for him. Not creepy ogling, but like a kind of soul food. So, instead of going on a cleaning frenzy, I lay on my side and pulled the covers down to show my "pleasantly plump" silhouette.

I also decided that whatever Chris wanted to do was ok.

If he wanted to stay mad all day, that was ok.

In the past, I would have taken responsibility for his anger.

If he wanted to stay mad today, that was on him, not on me.

As a King Day, it was his day to do with what he wished and desired.

I felt peace instead of the normal cleaning frenzy anxiety.

When Chris came out of the bathroom and saw me in bed, he softened.

Literally, his posture changed.

I went over and hugged him. I asked,

"Is there anything I can do for you?"

He hugged me back.

Then he cupped my jaw, kissed me, and whispered, "I want silence and snuggles in the morning. No words. On Queen Days, I'm happy to be buried in your words if that is what you desire."

Chris chose not to stay mad on his King Day.

There were dirty dishes left in the sink and dog fur clinging to the carpet...

And, most importantly, a happy King.

Don't worry if it takes a little time to get used to the role of servant and to prioritizing your partner all day long.

Here's the subtle and hard part to explain.

Because the King or Queen is in charge of their day, it's up to them to communicate their needs, wants, and desires clearly.

The role of the Dignified Servant of the Day is to SUPPORT and HELP the King/Queen achieve their needs, wants, and desires of that day.

The Servant of the Day is NOT RESPONSIBLE for those needs, wants, and desires.

The Queen/King does not get to blame or guilt the Servant of the Day for a "bad day." That "bad day" is entirely on the King or Queen's shoulders.

If you, as a servant, didn't hear or understand the request of the King or Queen, ask for clarification or a better way to communicate the requests.

If the Queen or King was clear and the Loyal Servant of the Day does not meet their needs, then a clarification of the servant role is in order.

That's all. It's not personal.

There is always another day to practice and get it right.

Once you read the next chapter, "Your Role as a Gracious Queen and King," you'll see why the Queen or King wouldn't dream of reprimanding a Loyal Servant of the Day. In fact, the role of the King and Queen has a bit of a surprising twist.

Your Role
as a Gracious Queen and King

This may sound strange or even counterintuitive....

The role of the gracious Queen or King is much like the role of a really good tour guide.

Imagine you are on a trip to an exotic place. You don't know the language, culture, expectations, and protocol of the land. You are in a different kingdom, so to speak.

Luckily, you are in the hands of a most excellent tour guide.

They want to share the beauty of their homeland and culture with you. They want you to see what they see and know what they know. They want you to understand the rules of their land so that you don't get into trouble.

More importantly, they want you to enjoy the rich landscape, the tantalizing flavors, the vibrant colors, and the alluring music of their country.

Much like an excellent tour guide, a gracious King or Queen shows their partner what they love, like, want, desire, abhor, enjoy, dislike, need, appreciate, and prefer in their kingdom.

This is a good time to mention that a trusted tour guide would never lead anyone to an unsafe or unwanted experience in their kingdom.

You may have heard the phrase, "with power comes responsibility." This applies within our partnerships.

The tour guide is patient, gracious, and enthusiastic when answering any questions the visitor may have.

To that end, the Queen or King's job is to:

1. Speak clearly about their needs and wants throughout their day.
2. Teach patiently over and over again, if needed.
3. Lead respectfully, by example.
4. Receive gratefully all of the acts of service offered by your partner.

Let me show you how each of these concepts played out over a Queen and King Day that happened several months into our royal days. We'd had a bit of practice by then....

It's 3:00 a.m.

I just couldn't sleep.

It's the wee hours of a Queen Day.

I'm sitting on the living room couch, wrapped in a blanket, quietly drinking a cup of tea.

I have SO much work to do. I'll be in my office all day.

Except here is the problem: I've been avoiding my office and my work.

I love lists of things to do and the feeling of accomplishing those things. Put a big green check mark next to a completed task and I'm a happy camper!

But lately, I barely get one task checked off my "to do" list.

What is going on?

I don't like being in my office, for one thing. Maybe I need to re-arrange it? *Hmmm*. Maybe the Feng Shui is all wrong? *Hmmm....*

I get out my laptop.

I start researching "Feng Shui office for success."

After four hours of research, I discover the Feng Shui in my office is ok, but the Feng Shui in Chris' office is a disaster!

I quietly crawl back into bed and snuggle up to Chris.

My head is spinning with the horrors of a misplaced office desk, blocked chi, stagnant energy, limited productivity, unbalanced elements, and dull wall colors that could lead to peril and doom!

Chris is still sleeping, blissfully unaware of the danger he is in.

We've got to re-arrange his office today! NOW!

His desk is facing away from his success corner. He can't go on this way! He's turning his back on opportunity! He's losing vital energy! He's going to die bitter and unfulfilled!

I take a deep breath.

I feel anxious. I hate feeling anxious.

I need to think.

There is another problem that needs to be addressed first.

Chris is not into this "woo-woo" stuff. He tries not to roll his eyes at me when I talk about astrology, past lives, energy work, spirits, and other metaphysical stuff. I have a reputation in my family as being "hippy woo-woo."

What can I say?

I went to a very, very liberal college. And, I grew up with a Native American grandmother who read swamp-tea leaves, told vivid stories about Cannibal Woman, Stick Indians, and Sasquatch, talked to spirits, and intuitively knew when people were coming to visit so she would head to the kitchen and start cooking salmon soup for the arriving guests.

I experienced things as a child, and young adult, that I could not begin to explain to my relatively conservative, church-going, white-collar, upper-middle-class, warm homemade chocolate chip cookies and milk after school husband.

Sigh.

But, still, the Feng Shui of his office had to be fixed immediately!

Chris' deep rhythmic breathing reminds me that there is yet a third problem.

Early in our marriage, I learned not to move, touch, or re-arrange any of Chris' stuff. It may look like a messy pile six feet high, but he knows exactly what is in each pile and where to find the script of a movie he worked on thirty years ago or the fourteen-year-old magazine article on the "10 Surprising Secrets to Unforgettable Stories."

This situation demands tact and diplomacy.

If that did not work, then a swift blow upside his head with my sovereign scepter should do the trick.

It's a Queen Day after all.

I snuggle into Chris and wait for him to wake up. I snuggle in some more…and some more….

He is still breathing heavily.

Hmmm…time to use some feminine wiles. I hold an awareness-inducing part of his anatomy.

Now he's stirring!

(I categorize use of feminine wiles under "tact and diplomacy." Some may use the word "manipulation." P*otato/Patahtoe*.)

It's ever so much easier to discuss touchy subjects when one is touching.

I tell Chris that I want to re-arrange his office today.

He is surprisingly receptive.

"You can move it all back if you don't like it," I promise.

"It's a Queen Day," he says wisely (also knowing that I love to re-arrange rooms), "whatever you want."

Two hours later, Chris is sitting behind his newly positioned desk facing his "success corner."

This is a position we would never have dreamed of putting his desk. Somehow it works beautifully. We move other pieces of furniture in his office. The room comes together like a stunning puzzle.

His space becomes a peaceful haven of vibrant creativity. You feel it when you step into the room.

Chris says, "I can actually breathe in here!"

That's about as close as he's ever come to admitting there may be something to this woo-woo stuff.

Chris happily helped me Feng Shui my office too. I'm loving my space and getting more work done!

Now is the time to introduce "phase two of woo."

A few days later, on a King Day, Chris and I are out shopping for the right curtains for his office. I mention that he is supposed to have some amethyst in his success corner.

"I don't know what amethyst is, but you're supposed to have some," I report. "I think it's a rock or crystal or something. There is a rock store in town. We could try there, if you want."

There is a *loooong* silence in the truck.

Neither of us ever considered rocks or crystals as anything other than pretty. It really does not matter to me if we go or not. And, it's a King Day. Chris is in charge of his day.

Chris says, "Why not? Let's quickly go there first."

Three hours later we step out of that rock shop with a whole bunch of beautiful stones, the amethyst, and something called a singing bowl.

We learned that a singing bowl is a metal bowl that when you rub a stick along the rim, it vibrates and hums. Much like rubbing your wet finger along a crystal glass.

Chris tried one of the singing bowls in the store. Every patron in the store stopped when the song of that bowl reverberated through the room. When the low vibration finally stopped, Chris said, "This is an old soul. This bowl is coming home with me."

Chris slid right into the WOO!

We had so much fun in that rock store. We were like kids let loose in a candy shop.

We were sharing something radically new and different together.

King and Queen Days were allowing us to open up to each other in ways we never would have done before.

In the past, Chris would not let me re-arrange his office or venture into a woo-woo shop with me.

There were subjects I would NEVER talk to Chris about, like crystals and Feng Shui. He would argue with me about their validity.

There were topics Chris didn't bring up around me, like politics. Apparently, I gave off the vibe that I thought his political views were stupid. (He's not wrong about that.)

This all changed.

Like a trusted tour guide, I got to show Chris parts of me (and my kingdom) he wouldn't have been open to before. As the Loyal Servant of the Day, he was willing to do whatever I wanted, even if it was woo-woo.

On King Days, Chris got to show me parts of himself (and his kingdom) I wouldn't have been open to before. As the Loyal Servant of the Day, I was willing to do whatever he wanted even if it involved going to some sort of fancy pants, outrageously expensive boat show in the city. (And actually having fun there too.)

We were growing together in ways we never dreamed possible all because we allowed ourselves to see each other's likes, wants, interests, and beliefs without judgement.

As a future Queen or King, what do you want to share with your Loyal Servant of the Day?

Royal Lexicon

In the spirit of having fun and sharing joy, Chris and I sometimes use fun language around our interactions.

We do this to diffuse arguments and call attention to behavior instead of personality.

If Chris is not being a particularly astute Loyal Servant of the Day, I may get his attention by saying, "Ahem!" and wait for him to realize that he's a bit out of line for his role of the day.

For more serious infractions, I may say, "The Queen is displeased." Though this may sound harsh, we both understand the spirit in which this is said, and it makes both of us smile. This is an example of a potential argument dissolved with fun language.

If, on a King Day, Chris has a full day of work, he may tell me that I am relieved of duty until 6:00. At which time, he will require my presence at dinner.

Here are some other royal phrases you can play with to help you diffuse arguments and make each other smile:

The Dignified Servant may say~

- What are your plans for the day and how may I be of assistance?
- May I...
- If it pleases his/her Majesty, I will...
- Is there anything your Majesty desires at this time?
- How may I be of service?
- When will you next require my presence?
- Shall I...
- As you wish.
- Would his/her Majesty like...
- How would his/her Majesty like me to proceed?
- I have twenty minutes until I have to leave, is there anything I can do for you?
- Very good.
- At your service.
- Whatever you desire.
- Would his/her majesty mind if I were to...?

The Queen or King may say~

- You are relieved of duty until...
- You are dismissed.
- The Queen/King expects you to...
- Disrobe.
- The Queen/King requires...
- The Queen/King desires...
- The Queen/King would like...

- It would please his/her Majesty to…
- That's not what the Queen/King desires.
- The Queen/King is displeased.
- The Queen/King is not amused.
- Pardon me?
- Proceed.
- Run along.
- Thank you, that will be all.
- Ahem!
- That's a command, not a request.

I hope you can see how these are meant to be lighthearted and fun. They are not to be spoken in harsh or mean-spirited tones.

Again, if the King/Queen and Servant titles do not float your boat, find titles that do inspire you. There are also other cultures to choose from as well; Tsar and Tsarina, Sultana and Sultan, Raha and Rani, Empress and Emperor….

Choose one and create your own lexicon.

Part of the goal is to see how often you can make your partner smile throughout the day. Language can be a big part of creating that joy.

Chris will explain in the next chapter how these Queen and King Days have transformed our marriage and brought so much more delight to our days.

The Royal Results...
Happily Ever After

Steph planted nasturtium seeds in the spring. The orange and yellow blossoms have taken over our garden.

Their bright green curly vines climb up the clumping bamboo forming what looks like six-foot-high arching nasturtium trees.

Who knew a few small seeds would create so much beauty?

That's what Steph and I thought about our silly little Queen and King Day experiment.

We now find ourselves more at ease with one another.

So many of our past resentments and conflicts have melted away.

We enjoy each other's company.

We explore our varied interests together.

We both have voice, choice, and equality.

I love Queen Days because I no longer have to wonder what Steph wants. I relax and let her take the lead.

Steph loves King Days because she gets to follow my lead. I let her know what I want.

She's responsible for her needs being met and I'm responsible for mine.

There is no place for unmet expectations and resentment.

It's pretty easy.

If one of us is holding a resentment, it's because we haven't asked for what we need and want. It's our own damn fault. It's impossible to blame our partner. We no longer hold tension around each other.

And, if there is ever any tension, we have our Queen or King Day to fix it.

After over a year of practicing King and Queen Days, Steph and I noticed that our King and Queen Days blurred together.

At some point, a shift occurred. Even on King Days, I would ask Steph if I could do anything for her. Steph also found herself asking me on Queen Days if there was anything she could do for me.

We both became so immersed in the habit of serving one another that, even on our own Queen or King Days, we would ask if there was anything we could do for one another.

Today, Steph and I rely less and less on the structure of King and Queen Days. Our days tend to meld into Royal Couple Days of genuine service, mutual hospitality, kindness, and equality.

This simple practice of daily generosity created a tenderness and *companionability* that simply did not exist between us before.

I'm grateful for that moment when something prompted me to say, "I want to serve you like a Queen"—and mean it!

And Steph will admit, Queenship suits her.

Perhaps Queenship and Kingship will suit you too.

The next chapter shows you how to begin your own royal journey.

Getting Started on
Your Own Royal Journey

Let's get you started on the royal road to a happier marriage.

Surprise! You are already on your royal way.

In an earlier chapter, you asked your partner if there is anything you can do for them. Right?

Let's build on that.

I'm going to make an assumption here. You are reading this book hoping your partner will want to join you in this royal experiment.

So, the first thing to do is invite them to join you on this journey.

Ask your partner if they would be willing to try this for one day. Make them the boss of the day. Let them know you would like to serve them all day, however they desire.

Use the 10 words, "I want to serve you…you know, like a Queen/King."

What if they refuse your offer? Read below. We've got you covered.

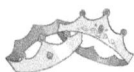

If your partner is not willing to join you on this royal journey, try this:

Start the journey anyway.

Treat your partner like royalty the next day anyway. But, don't tell them what you are doing. Do what Chris did. From the moment you get up in the morning to the moment you go to sleep, practice genuine service. Ask, "Is there anything I can do for you?"

Whether or not your partner wants to play, you can be the best partner possible. Be the shiny example in your marriage. Watch yourself though. You must be able to do this without resentment or any hidden expectations. Here is where you do NOT follow Chris' example. (Remember when he threw the tizzy fit? Don't do that.)

Take it one day at a time.

You may notice your partner begin to soften. They will

start to rely on you, trust you, and look forward to being with you.

Once they've felt the effects of your attention, ask them again if they will join you on this journey.

Chris recommends saying something like this:

> "Honey, I would love to take a day with you. I want to prioritize you. I want you to feel prioritized. I want to treat you like a King/Queen. I want you to know that I love you and I want you to feel loved. What can I do for you on that day so that you KNOW you are loved?"

If your partner say yes to this and you get to enjoy this day together, ask them if they would be willing to do the same for you?

Now that your partner is willing to join you, decide who's going to play the role of royalty first.

When it is your turn to be the Dignified Servant of the Day, ask your partner, "Is there anything I can do for you?" This question should be asked within the first few minutes of the King/Queen waking up.

If he or she answers, "No thanks," offer coffee or breakfast in bed.

Then put into practice what you have learned in this book. Here are the steps and guidelines from previous chapters:

Follow the 5 steps:

1. Check in With Your Partner
2. Help Your Partner Get What They Need and Want
3. Ask for What You Need and Want
4. Take Turns Giving and Receiving
5. Reduce Arguments by Using Fun Ways to Think About Each Other

And,

Be an awesome Dignified Servant of the Day:

1. Check in at the beginning of the day to find out the King/Queen's plans for the day.
2. Knowing the plans, find ways to make the day go as smoothly as possible.
3. Check in throughout the day to see if there is anything to do to make the King/Queen's day even better.
4. Notice surprising and fun ways to go above and beyond to delight the King or Queen.
5. Check in at the end of the day to see if there is anything else needed or wanted.

And then,

Be an excellent Gracious Queen or King:

1. Speak clearly about your needs and wants throughout the day.

2. Teach patiently over and over again if needed.
3. Lead respectfully, by example.
4. Receive gratefully all of the acts of service offered by your partner.

Most importantly, have fun!

Then, switch and try for one more day.

You may ask, "How do I know if this Royal Couple thing is working?"

Well, do you or your spouse feel warmer, softer, and more open to one another?

Do you or your partner find yourself trusting each other more?

Are you leaning into one another?

Are you wanting to be around each other more?

Do you feel like you can breathe better?

Then it's working!

Chris and I noticed a huge shift within the first two weeks of alternating between King and Queen Days. Once we got through those first two weeks, it became very natural to continue.

So, try it for 14 days.

If you would like extra help, and to hear more stories of how we handled those first couple of weeks, go to: royalcouple.com/14days.

Also...

Let us know how your first 14 days go.

1. What was most surprising for you?
2. What was harder than you expected?
3. Which role was more challenging for you?
4. What was your biggest mess up?
5. When did you shine?
6. How did your partner surprise or delight you?
7. Which sticky arguments dissolved?
8. What was the most fun for you?

Email me at: steph@royalcouple.com

Chris and I can't wait to hear from you!

Questions

&

Answers

What if my partner is not a good servant?

The first question to ask is, were you clear about your wants, needs, and expectations for the day?

If so, is your partner stressed or otherwise distracted?

For example, when Chris' dad was really ill, Chris was not able to be present for me on Queen Days. I didn't expect him to be available. I wasn't angry or upset. There were other priorities at that time.

On the other hand, on one King Day, I was really stressed about a situation at work. Chris was upset with me for not being present for him. He let me know. I still was not able to pull it together for him. He later came and apologized. Even though it was a King Day, he realized that I was not able to show up for him. He gave me grace. We call this, "a royal pardon."

Some days are going to be like that.

Or perhaps your partner is intimidated by the loss of control. They may need to be in the Queen or King seat for a few more days. They might need to see how you are an excellent Loyal Servant of the Day. Chris had to do this for me. I needed lots of practice being a good Dignified Servant of the Day. I'm so glad Chris was patient with me. It paid off for him. Trust me.

What if my partner asks me to do something I don't want to do?

My first response is don't do it! If your gut says NO, then NO it is. QUEEN AND KING DAYS ARE NOT A PLATFORM FOR ABUSE OF ANY KIND!

That said, a few questions you can ask yourself are:

1. Why am I resisting?
2. Why is this uncomfortable?
3. What am I afraid of?
4. What's the worst that can happen?

I personally did encounter the pole-dancing-with-bacon fear and the being-devoured fear. I stepped into those and discovered my fears were unfounded. What I did find was a kind and sweet husband. I leaned into those fears and grew.

This is an excellent time to listen to your inner wisdom. It's there, waiting to guide you.

And, this is a good time to note that King and Queen Days are not meant as days to shove a "Honey Do List" at your partner. The point is genuine service, trust, and fun, remember? If Queen and King Days are all about drudgery, then, what's the joy in that?

There was one Queen Day when I asked Chris to help me work on the house. This was right before an appraisal for a re-finance. I gave him plenty of notice and listed the four specific tasks I needed help with. I personally LOVE making the house cleaner and more efficient. It was a treat for me to get these things accomplished on my day, but I certainly don't make a habit of a "Honey Do List."

What if we just don't have the time to do this? We're so busy!

Couples with full-time jobs and young children might find this harder to implement to the extent Chris and I did to begin with.

There are still small opportunities to use this in your day!

How much time does it take to simply stop and ask, "Is there anything I can do for you right now?" Maybe the simple answer in that moment is, "Yes, can you please give Timmy a glass of milk?" or "Yes, can you just give me fifteen minutes to sit quietly before we make dinner?"

Sometimes, I think we're afraid of the answer to the question, "Is there anything I can do for you?" We are worried the answer will take a huge amount of time or effort when we are already feeling overloaded.

Try it anyway. See where and how you can fit a few precious moments into your day. Moments where you can be of simple service to your partner. Begin with easy acts of service and agree to communicate if something feels overwhelming.

Start small.

Sometimes the question, "What can I do for you?" simply shows support. Sometimes in a hectic, overwhelming day, that's all we need to know that we are supported.

What happens when I want to schedule something for myself on my partner's royal day?

This happens to Chris and me all of the time.

To begin with, Chris and I stick to our original King and Queen Days no matter what.

Early in our King/Queen day experiment, there was a week where all of the family and work obligations fell on my Queen Days. All of the King Days were free of obligations. Chris kindly offered to swap out one of his King Days for a Queen Day so that I could have a proper Queen Day. Even though this seemed to make a lot of sense, we agreed not to switch Queen and King Days for two reasons:

1. This could become very difficult to keep track of.
2. The expectation would be planted that a difficult day should be traded out. That leads to more arguments, resentments, and *ick*.

We understand that some weeks are better for the Queen and some weeks are better for the King.

We trust that it will balance out in the end.

With that in mind, if I have an opportunity to plan an event on a Queen Day (my day), I might say to Chris, "Hey, my mom just invited me to visit Aunt Suzy on Thursday. I'd like to go. You are relieved of duty on Thursday night. Have fun!"

If that same opportunity came on a King day, I'll say, "I know Thursday is a King Day and we have the evening open. I was just invited by my mom to go visit Aunt Suzy. I'd like to go if you don't have any huge plans."

Most of the time Chris will reply, "Sure, that sounds like fun. But, keep the next King Day open. I have plans for you...."

Chris prioritizes Queen Days the same way.

To be honest, it's weird to ask permission from someone else to do something. Chris and I had to be really careful here. Too much control leads to resentments and mistrust. I've only been resentful at Chris once for "denying" me the opportunity to do something. I don't remember exactly what it was but, I do remember it was for a good reason.

Find more resources on the next page.

Resources

Put what you just learned into practice!

Let us walk you through your first two weeks. Check out the *14-Day Marriage Reset*. You will get extra help, guidelines, prompts, and more stories of how Chris and I quickly overcame obstacles in our marriage.

https://RoyalCouple.com/14days

Want more? Check out the Royal Couple website where you will find ways to pamper each other and other resources at:

https://RoyalCouple.com/resources

Read *Royal Couple* with your book club friends! Explore lively relationship questions and topics here:

https://RoyalCouple.com/bookclub

Acknowledgments

We would like to thank all of you who joined us on this royal journey. Those of you who listened, laughed, encouraged, read various drafts of this book, and were candid about your marriages.

Thank you for your courage and honesty.

About the Authors

Steph and Chris have been married for 27 years, parenting for 19 years, in business together for 12 years, and they actually love being together (now that they are a Royal Couple).

Chris and Steph also produce, in partnership with many stellar colleagues and outstanding companies, the annual Nonprofit Storytelling Conference (and other online and in-person trainings) that equip nonprofit organizations from all over the world to expand their capacity to serve others.

Whenever possible, Steph and Chris round up as many family and friends as they can and sneak away to their favorite lake for camping, boating, storytelling, and s'mores under the stars. They live in wet and wonderful Washington State with their two adventurous teenage boys, two affectionate dogs, and an ancient cat.